THE STREETS

THE

21ST

CENTURY

EGYPT

BREAKING FREE FROM AN AGE-OLD SYSTEM

DEMOND MILLS

LOVE CLONES
publishing

Love Clones Publishing
www.lcpublishing.net

First Printing, 2016

ISBN: 978-0692618585

King James Version Scripture quotations marked "KJV" are taken from the Holy Bible, King James Version (Public Domain).

New King James Version Scripture quotations marked "NKJV" are taken from the New King James Version. Copyright © 1982 by Thomas Nelson, Inc. Used by permission. All rights reserved.

Publishers:
Love Clones Publishing
Dallas, TX 75205
www.lcpublishing.net

DEDICATION

To my Lord and Savior Jesus Christ, I'd like to give you all the honor for the revelation that you poured into me through Your Spirit. Thank you for leading and guiding me to words of truth, for the truth will set the reader free.

To my Rib, my loving wife Debra, I thank God for you each and every day. He that finds a wife finds a good thing and receives favor from God. I found my good and God has favored me with two beautiful children. I love you guys and your love keeps me balanced.

To my brothers and sisters, since the day I dedicated my life to Christ, I've always thought about how to be a good example to you by walking in the love of Christ. I lay my life down so that you can live a better life. I love you with the love of Christ.

To my mother, I would like to thank you for your prayers. I thank God for your love and support. You are a great mother and I love you with an everlasting love.

My covering, Apostle Kevin and Candace Ford. My life has thrust in so many ways through the consistency of your out pouring of love. You are truly an example of what it means to be spiritual parents. Your life exemplifies inspiration and true character.

INTRODUCTION

Misery is related to the word (downer), which means to relax or get comfortable.

You may be one of many throughout the world who thinks that God has forgotten about them. You may constantly wonder why bad things continue to happen to you and why it seems as though you can't get a breakthrough. Let me tell you, God is not ignoring you; He is on your side. He has seen how you are suffering and the misery it is causing you.

The devil wants you to suffer in order for you to become and stay miserable. God has seen what Egypt and the Egyptians are doing to you. The Egyptians are slave drivers according to the scriptures. Have you noticed times in your life, that the things you use to say no to, stand up to and have control over are now uncontrollable?

You find yourself being driven by things instead of being led. The enemy's desire is to take control of your life and drive you into a life of misery.

*T**he Lord said," I have seen the misery of my people in Egypt. I have heard them crying out because of their slave drivers, And I am concerned about their suffering, so I have come down to rescue them from the hands of the Egyptians and bring them up and out of that land into a good spacious land, a land flowing with milk and honey the home of the Canaanites, Hittites, Amorites, Perizzites, Hivites and Jebusites -Exodus 3:7-8***

The longer you stay in Egypt, the more you get relaxed and comfortable. So God is coming down to help you move up and out of Egypt. So you don't have to accept the life that brings misery. Rather it's a relationship, job or living condition, you were made to be stress free, worry free and enjoy life. It's time to get your freedom back with the help of God; you can come up and out of your circumstance.

Up is defined as from a lower to higher place or position upward from the ground or surface so as to expose a particular surface into possession or custody being the one whose turn it is.

In order for God to bring you out of a situation, He must bring you up from a lower place to a higher position. As long as you stay in misery, you will never receive your place and position. God wants to move you from operating through your five senses and bring you into revelation or the ability to discern the true colors of your enemy. As long as you stay in Egypt, you will always walk in your flesh and become immune to your surroundings. God wants to expose the surface of Egypt to you, so that you can take possession and custody over your enemy.

*H*e replied, " I saw Satan fall like lightning from heaven. I have given you authority to trample on snakes and scorpions and to overcome all the power of the enemy; nothing will harm you. At that time Jesus full of joy through the Holy Spirit said; I praise you Father lord of heaven and earth because you have hidden these things from the wise and learned and revealed them to little children. -Luke 10:18, 21*

God will give you power over Egypt and from being deceived by snakes and scorpions. In Genesis 3, the serpent came to confuse Eve with deception. Scorpions are creatures that strikes it's enemy with a pointed tale called a stinger. It injects poison in order to paralyze its victims. The enemy will use a scorpion spirit to paralyze you. In your mind you see yourself walking with potential but outwardly you can't seem to walk away. This is the reality of what you see many people struggling to overcome in life. God has given you authority and power to overcome all the power of the streets -

J *esus replied Blessed are you Simon son of Jonah, for this was not revealed to you by man but by my father in heaven and I tell you that you are Peter and on this rock I will build my church*

and the gates of hades will not overcome it. -
Matthew 16:17-18

So we fix our eyes not on what we see in the flesh but on what is unseen, through revelation. For what is seen, living in misery, is temporary, but what is unseen is eternal, God's plan for your life. Choosing to see a thing differently doesn't mean you are in denial, it just means that you would rather look at things differently. You can fix your circumstance with your eyes. The enemy of the streets doesn't want you to fix your eyes on what you discern spiritually but rather his plan is to keep you focused on what's in front of you, which is the streets.

We all know someone in our life who can't seem to see outside of the streets (Egypt) no matter how many times they are presented with a better option in life. You put a choice before them and they will choose sagging pants over a suit and tie. They fix their eyes on things that are seen and not on things they don't experience often which is a suit and tie. Circumstances we experience through our five senses are to be temporary and not a struggle!

People tend to develop temporary behaviors and beliefs. Money is temporary in the streets; relationships are temporary in the streets like a season that changes. I have come in contact with many people that stop praying and believing God. God is good only when things are going well in their life. However, when the pressure of life comes knocking at their door and they are in need of results, they tend to rely on temporary answers.

*W*hen the people saw that Moses was so long in coming down from the mountain, they gathered around Aaron and said, come make us a god who will go before us. As for this fellow Moses who brought us up out of Egypt, we don't know what happen to him. -Exodus 32:1*

Stay committed to prayer because God is committed to answer you! When it seems like prayer is taking too long many people relapse and begin to take off all they have accomplished and twist the word of God.

I grew up with friends who knew the scriptures very well. I thought that nothing and no one would be able to convince them from changing their beliefs. When I talk to them today most of what was revelation has now been transformed into man made rules, twisted scriptures, religion and tradition. Bad company will rust out your faith walk. All it takes is one person to start a trend and the more you stay around them, the more convincing you'll become at believing that "Moses" is taking too long with an answer from God. The Moses of today is our church leader or an individual in which we admire.

BREAKING OLD AGE HABITS

_____

_____

_____

_____

_____

_____

_____

_____

_____

_____

_____

_____

_____

_____

CHAPTER 1

*F*or he has rescued us from the dominion of darkness and brought us into the kingdom of his son he loves -Colossians 1:13

The modern day Egypt is the streets! It's very dark and people throughout the world are being dominated by the power of darkness in the streets. The longer you stay in dark places the more you lose vision. What seems easy to see will be hard to avoid. Have you ever tried to walk in your house with the lights off but bumped into an object or knocked things over. It's the same way in the streets; you will bump into people places and things, discovering littering everywhere because no one wants to take responsibility for their own action but would rather point the finger at the next person.

There is hoarding throughout the streets, which suggest that individuals are holding on to unforgiveness. In the streets it's a struggle to let go of what someone did to you and to forgive them. When you choose not to forgive others it will gradually cause a person to build a wall up. In this dark place you will find yourself grabbing the wall for guidance and support. You will reach for familiar things to help steer you where you need to go but will find your self-walking in the fruit of your flesh. We must turn on the light switch so we can see what to stay away from and avoid.

John 8:12, when Jesus spoke again to the people, he said, " I am the light of the world. Whoever follows me will never walk in darkness, but will have the light of light.

No matter how things may appear, Jesus is the light switch of your life. When you turn on the lights in a house it allows you to see what belongs to you. A person can live their entire life without an identity. Without knowing what they can possess. The devil does not want you to discover who you are or find a way out of the streets. He wants to strip you down and take away anything that will give you access to God. His plan is to steal your prayer life, your belief in God, your faith, your hearing, your vision and most of all your fellowship with God.

The enemy will constantly approach you

with deception until there's nothing left to fight him off. He relentlessly approached Eve until her and Adam surrendered.

After this I looked and there before me was a door standing open in heaven. And the voice I heard speaking to me like a trumpet said, Come up here (revelation) and I will show you what must take place after this (coming out of Egypt). At once I was in the spirit (revelation) and there before me was a throne in heaven with someone sitting on it. Revelation 4:1-2

The streets will beat you down and cause you to lose your self-esteem. You will walk with your head down feeling like all eyes are on you. You will find it difficult to smile at others as you pass them by. The prom queen may not look the same any more; she's gained weight, lost her hair, got on drugs and lost her children because of her addiction. The most popular guy in school who you thought would become successful has lost everything and is now living on the streets homeless with no money. Family and friends look down on him as if he's a lost cause or like a disease that is contagious. When you mention their name people begin to say, "stay away from him, her or them" because being around them will get you in trouble. It's true being in certain circumstances can lead to habitual behavior. You can quickly go from an honor roll behavior to an alternative behavior.

Merriam-Webster definition for alternative not usual or traditional, other words people attend to stray away from the traditional.

Habits that we learned from our parents. We have all had different upbringings but we all have one thing in common and that is to have "RESPECT". I remember times when brothers and sisters never crossed the line by calling each other out their name. When there was a disagreement, siblings would talk it out and come to terms by accepting responsibility for their action. It was the traditional way to show each other respect there was no alternative way but to show each other respect.

Perhaps your self-esteem was lost because of bad decision in life by committing crimes, even after many years of staying crime free society seems to remind you of your wrong doing by rejecting you of a new beginning.

The enemy wants you to have a low self-esteem. Low self-esteem is designed to keep you focused on "dressing down" rather than "dressing up" for confidence. Meditation and prayer will help build your confidence. In Revelation 4:1 there is a door open for you to walk through regardless of the mistakes you made in life. The doors you will see is God's way of letting you know that his arms are open to receive you no matter what you have done. God will open doors for you that no man can shut!

In God's arm you can rest and He will read a story to you like a parent who reads a story to their child. The story is about how great you are and how you were made to win. However, if you don't learn how to come up higher in your thinking then you will always remain not knowing who you are or who has the final say so in your life.

BREAKING OLD AGE HABITS

_____

_____

_____

_____

_____

_____

_____

_____

_____

_____

_____

_____

_____

_____

CHAPTER 2

In Revelation 1:10 John heard a voice that sounded like a trumpet. A trumpet is used as order and to demand attention. God is looking to get your attention by revealing His Word to you. The word of God is meant to draw your attention and change your posture. You will learn how to stand up straight with your head up high when you attend to the word. John saw a door open but he had to come up higher, expand his mind, his eyes, his hearing and his language to another level. You can't be afraid of height if you want to go to the next level. You can't be afraid to leave the ground of the streets while expecting a better life.

In Revelation chapter four, Jesus says to

John come up here and I will show you what's to come. John saw a throne with one sitting on it. God wants you to see that He still exists and still sits on his throne as God almighty.

In the midst of trials and tribulation you must continue to believe that God still sits on his throne as Lord over your life. God wants to be the head of your life and not the tail of your life. The first choice should always be God; He should never come second when you are in need of help.

When your head is down you look at things downward or decline. You will start to believe the enemy's presentation and except his proposal. The more you continue to look downward the further you will be from God and your relationship with him. The enemy knows that his time is running out so he is trying to recruit as many people as he can to be with him in hell. Just because the devil lost his relationship with God, doesn't mean you have to. Having a relationship with God is key especially when you need guidance. Spending time with God will strengthen you and give you confidence.

You will walk with your head up high and not slump down. You will look up as with a reverent respect to God as a way to say to Him that I choose you first or turn to you first and not as a second option.

When you lose your self-esteem you feel uncomfortable and naked. Adam felt naked and without covering. He lost his confidence and his covering, God Almighty. God has covered you and protected you with his love. There are those in this world who look for love in the wrong places and do it out of the wrong reasons. They saw fig trees as a way to lean towards the world rather than leaning on God for comfort.

According to the Merriam-Webster dictionary the meaning of a fig leaf -something that prevents embarrassment or criticism by covering or hiding something. A fig leaf is also known for providing natural treatment to sickness or skin problems. So many people are looking for the streets to treat their skin problems. They cover up the pain, hurt and put on a false wardrobe, while deep inside they are in pain. No matter how many leaves a person uses it will never erase the hurt and pain. Like a leaf when seasons change, people's ways change colors and soon fall off the tree. Your leaf may appear green now with the most vibrant colors but soon when the weather of life changes, it will fade away showing your true colors. During the fall season you always see leaves drying up and then falling off the trees. Understand this, the leaf you put your trust in will fall off and expose the branches and barks. Branches are an extension from the tree; you will be amazed to find out how much things are connected to each other.

I no longer call you servants, because a servant does not know his masters business, instead I have called you friends, for everything that I learned from my father I have made known to you. You did not choose me, but I have choose you and appointed you so that you might go and bear fruit, fruit that will last and that whatever you ask in my name the father will give you. -John 15:15-16

The word *chose* in this verse comes from the Greek word (eko-gomai) means to select, make a choice, choose (out), chosen; other related word is lego which means to break silence or to name. Growing up as a kid one of the most popular toys were Legos. What is so fascinating about this toy is that you learn how to put pieces together making it whatever you want it to be. You are able to add on or take off accordingly. Jesus "lego" us by rebuilding our lives by adding what we need and subtracting what we don't. We were broken up into many pieces but Jesus put our lives back together again to make us whole. It is finished and now it's time to introduce you to the world as the new and improve YOU!

Have you ever seen a makeover show? Some of the contestants need an entirely new set up teeth because their teeth are decayed or missing or filled with cavities. No matter how bad the condition is of their teeth, there seems to still be hope for newly created mouth. When God makes you new He gives you a new mouth changing your unclean language to appropriate language. It's not what you say, but how you say it.

People will tend to bring the streets to a job and expect others to relate. Being a manager at my job gives me the advantage to help many men by teaching them how to be appropriate in the corporate arena when they come to be interviewed. Immediately, I look past their mistakes and focus on how I can get them to see money different from how the street views money. Gradually I give them nuggets on how to have a blue collar on wherever they go. I often help them in the makeover process by reminding them to keep their pants pulled up.

Unfortunately, to them they believe that sagging pants is a "blue collar' because that is their norm. The world identifies a suit and tie as a form of business or the streets identify name brand clothes as a suit and jewelry as a tie. Egypt is a place of fantasies and deception.

BREAKING OLD AGE HABITS

_____

_____

_____

_____

_____

_____

_____

_____

_____

_____

_____

_____

_____

CHAPTER 3

gain the devil took him to a very high mountain and showed him all the splendor. All this I will give you, "he said, if you bow down and worship me." Matthew 4:8-9

The devil was trying to deceive Jesus. He wanted Him to accept the fantasies with thoughts of this world (high mountain). Fantasying is one of the devil tactics he uses to get a person into a world called, "what would it be like?" You will play dress rehearsal in your mind with your imagination of "what would it be like to?" It's like a rollercoaster ride with thrills and excitement. As a teenager I was fascinated with the suit and ties of the streets.

34

Life wasn't always peaches and cream for me growing up. The devil told Jesus that he would give him all the splendor of this world if he bowed down to him. The devil was actually saying, "sale your identity to me for this temporary enjoyment". He wanted Jesus to make him his idol. We become tempted to want what others have.

The things you see growing up in the neighborhood, are what draws you to idolize it at a young age. There was generally someone in our lives who we liked to imitate, either because of the way they dressed or the car they drove. I was fascinated in what my uncle Charles wore and drove. I recall one time he let me sit in his car. I got behind the steering wheel and began to imagine what it would be like to drive a car like his. He was known for driving Cadillacs and would change his cars like people changed their clothes.

Even though I couldn't drive that didn't stop my mind from imagining. Sitting in his car was the high mountain and through it I was able to see the splendor or glamour that comes with having a fancy car.

Worldly popularity is short term. The same people who voted you in can vote you out of popularity. Having the best clothes or car doesn't keep you on top; there is always something else that will catch people's attention. I always thought the Cadillac was the ultimate car until I saw other luxury vehicles. People get caught up in wanting to be like the next person but don't consider what path they chose to have the same things in life. The one you look up to perhaps could make a living by gambling, drug trafficking, robbing, or lying on others just to get ahead in life or backstabbing. These are just a few roads that some travel down to obtain material things. Why would you want to have what others have when our Heavenly Father has already chosen a prosperous path for you and no one can travel on it but you?

Have you ever heard the saying, " it's easy to get in trouble but hard to get out of it"? Someone else's road may look easy to travel but can be hard to get out of. People are getting lost in the world and can't seem to find a way out. God has predestined a path for you to travel on where you will never get lost. Have you noticed that when a person gets lost, only a few will fight the odds to survive or live, that's because they realize this is not how their life should end. When someone gets lost usually they recalculate their steps by identifying checkpoints. If you haven't found the way out maybe it's because you can't remember if how you got to that point in the first place. Survivors will find their way to a road and flag down any passing vehicle for help. God is waiting for you to reach the nearest road in life and flag Him down for help.

And God heard their groaning, and God remembered His covenant with Abraham, with Isaac, and with Jacob. -Exodus 2:24

Regrettably, too many people stay quiet and won't talk about the hurt or pain they are feeling, they'd rather keep it bottled up inside and expect others to play hide and seek. The streets will bring you nothing but hurt and pain. When you are taught to suck it up and get over it, how can one get over from being molested, rapped, or physical and verbal abused while being told to never tell anyone about their experience? It takes years sometimes to open up about your experience in life. God heard the Israelites groaning and remembered His covenant.

Webster definition of groaning means to make a deep moan because of pain or some strong emotion to say something that expresses unhappiness to complain about something.

You've been burying this pain for too long

and now its rooted deep issues that need to be released. Just like God heard the cries of the Israelites, He is also waiting to hear from you. A closed mouth can't be fed, the Israelites were burying all that hurt and pain. When you make your mind up that you will survive, you will do whatever it takes to find the nearest road out of Egypt and make your voice heard with groaning that can be heard!

*E*nter through the narrow gate. For wide is the gate and broad is the road that Leads to destruction, and many enter through it. But small is the gate and narrow the Road that leads to life, and only a few find it. Matthew 7:13-14 (NIV)

There are many people who confide in the

wrong people and it becomes a nightmare. You may think that friends can be trusted but the truth of the matter is that is not always the case. What I am saying is close friends can be like a broad road that can lead to destroying a person when that friend should be uplifting. Trusting our friends or love ones is traditional and that's okay but we must be careful whose gate we enter in or open up to.

According to the Merriam-Webster Dictionary, broad means large from one side to the other side having a specified width: including or involving many things or people.

When told to the wrong person, a conversation can end up wide open with the middle left out. People like to leave out information and before you know it, he said becomes she said! He said, she said, they said, we said, is how stories get half told and opens the door for gossip. How many times have you heard an incomplete story? How wide was the space in between? In Egypt everyone enjoys the demise of someone who makes mistakes in life. They become the talk of the town or gossip to others. The more the story spreads the more it will become disconnected from the truth There is an old saying, "connect the dots". What that means is keep the story attached and not gapped with bits and pieces of the puzzle.

One piece missing from a puzzle can end up destroying someone's life. A picture of you has been part of the puzzle that makes you complete. This is how people's character is assassinated. The streets will cut you into pieces and leave you for dead. Liars will lure you into a pit of lions hoping that you lose your mind with thoughts that you just can't stop thinking about. The longer you stay there the more you become afraid of what people think of you. Fear is like a bully that desires to keep you from coming forward with what has devastated and hindered you for years.

People in the streets prey over weakness and will take advantage over you. Women across the world struggle with their identity and men are afraid to show gentleness or embrace humility. The wall gets tougher to break and grows higher to keep trespassers out. Let go and let God in! If you are stepping forward then you have to exit out of your past and enter into your future.

Very truly I tell you, whoever hears my word and believes him who sent me has eternal life and will not be judged but has crossed over from death to life. -John 5:24 (NIV)

Forget about your past, everything in it is dead. Everything before you is alive! You've been listening to the wrong advice, now it's time to listen to God. Sometimes we get advice from those who haven't dealt with their own issues. Their advice is like a transferring of spirits, that's looking for a place to recycle feelings. They themselves are victims and still haven't been delivered yet.

When I started dating many of my friends would try to give me advice on my relationship.

It seemed reasonable to listen to what they had to say since we were friends. I accepted every piece of advice hoping to get as many women I could get in the bed. After a while I noticed that I was becoming their story of tales in the hood.

This is how a person's reputation gets tainted with rumors, especially women. I finally came across a woman who I'd known since childhood. Every time we would cross paths we would joke around and make each other's day. We had a dance off in our junior high school party and to this day we still enjoy that memory. As time passed I didn't see her anymore. One day while I was sitting at home the phone rang when I answered it I heard a voice say, "Devo?" I knew it was her because she always called me by that name. That day we picked up from where we left off and soon our friendship turned into something other than just friends.

When you find a woman that you think is easy to get over on, make sure that your facts are straight not bits and pieces of her life. I truly thought that she would easily take off her clothes off for me, from the rumors that I'd heard. Yet, the approach I used numerous times on other females didn't work on her. What I learned was that you can't judge a book by its cover. That was nearly twenty years ago and I can proudly say it was worth waiting for because she is my wife today.

So many individuals have been hurt from a variety of different ways that we couldn't imagine. These days you will hear about someone getting hurt by the church. I know you're probably saying to yourself that the church is a hospital. Yet the truth of the matter is some churches can be a reflection of Egypt. You shouldn't attend church AND be in bondage. That's the reason why you go to church, to break free from the Egyptians.

Pharaohs are in the pulpits shooting arrows at the congregation, acting like he was preaching the word. He abuses you with slavery and no opportunity. You building for him a city, but have no invitation to come in. When Moses approached Pharaoh he came with some revelation but Pharaoh tried to convince him to believe in magic or be controlled by mind control. Thank God for revelation, through it we learn our true identity. We get comfortable in going to church and sitting on our gifts. A church that is ran like Egypt can bring you misery. You get comfortable, so God is coming to help you come up and out of misery through revelation.

Breaking Old Age Habits

_____

_____

_____

_____

_____

_____

_____

_____

_____

_____

_____

_____

_____

_____

CHAPTER 4

It is very hot in Egypt with little shade. The temperature is scorching hot and muggy. You're looking for shade but the chances are slim. As you search for water you become more and more dehydrated. This is how many people feel today. Some churches have no shade or say they provide covering for those who are dehydrated. That's why you are burnt out. The water you receive is limited. Just like plants need water to grow, we all need the water of encouragement to excel.

Sadly, water is not clean in Egypt but it's hazardous to your health. What I mean is that it's hard for you to be acknowledged for any achievements. If you get a new car people's attitude towards you changes. If you start dressing differently from other than the streets, people feel like you think your better than the next person. Every time you take a step forward someone is always trying to push you back into bondage.

The limitation of water supply will make any group of people fight for a drink. What I mean is that the streets Is a place where men and woman are fighting over relationships. Everyone is looking for love in all the wrong places, just THIRSTY. When you think that you are the only one who was intimate with a certain person the chances are slim of you being the only one. To your surprise the boundaries have been moved and it could be your best friend, next door neighbor or one of your family members. The thirst is real with no resistance and many find out that after all that rotation that you may be sleeping with a family member (incest).

Imagination grows significant in Egypt for a lack of places to go. You must keep in mind that the Israelites were in bondage with limited access to any activity. What I mean is that children as well adults have to do with what they got by making up places to go or games to play house. Now I know you're probably saying different nationalities do the same thing, that may be true but in the streets we can we can cross the line and before you know it our children end up experiencing sexual behavior.

At a young age we pick up on things like sponges. The streets become what they see on a regular basis. I truly believe that this is how the imagination grows. Imagination is like a form of witchcraft. You can't think for yourself, you seem to not understand why you keep going back to the same man after he or she has cheated or verbal and physical abuse.

We are taught to believe in all kinds of old wives tales. We become very superstition. When we break something especially glass our first reaction is I have seven years of bad luck. Breaking glass has nothing to do with having a rough time in life or had a rough day at work. We all will have some trying days but I guarantee you that it will have nothing to do with a breaking of some glass.

Another familiar wives tale is "bread and butter". Bread and butter is a superstition blessing or charm, typically said by young couples or friends walking together when they are forced to separate bad luck of letting something come between them to be averted.

How about sweeping over some one's feet you will have bad luck or never get married. Another one is if a black cat crosses your path you will have seven years of bad luck. How about if you step on a crack you will break your mothers back. All of these represent divination or a form of witchcraft.

BREAKING AGED OLD SYSTEMS

1. Think of a wives tale and name it.
2. Did any of the superstition bring you bad luck?
3. Do you still believe in them today?
4. Identify it and break all soul ties to it.

BREAKING OLD AGE HABITS

_____

_____

_____

_____

_____

_____

_____

_____

_____

_____

_____

_____

_____

_____

CHAPTER 5

The thirst is real with all kinds of creatures alike such as leeches. Leeches are a parasite that clings on to things by sucking blood. What I mean is that some people behaviors are like a leech. Everyone is looking for a come up. They are looking for opportunity; we call them opportunist.

It seems like when you trying to get ahead in life a leech comes along and want any extras. It's okay to help those in need I'm not talking about them but that sister, brother, cousin or friend. Make it out of the hood and watch the leeches come from afar; it will be people who you haven't seen in years.

No matter where you go you will find reptiles, some small and some great. You can't trust anyone with confidential information. They like to slither their way around ready to boa constrict you by wrapping involving you in mess. You'll find yourself in the middle of things because the snake lied on you. When they speak venom is release out their mouth by injecting people with lies.

You will also come across ponds with frogs hopping from one place to another. What I mean is that hopping representing jumping from place to place. This behavior expresses that a person is uncertain about things in life or just can't make their mind up. So they hop from church to church and from one relationship to another.

BREAKING AGED OLD SYSTEM

1. Do you find yourself not being able to get ahead in life?
2. Identify the leech in your life.
3. Do you find yourself in the middle of gossip?
4. Do you have a problem with making a decision?

BREAKING OLD AGE HABITS

_____

_____

_____

_____

_____

_____

_____

_____

_____

_____

_____

_____

_____

_____

ABOUT THE AUTHOR

Born and raised in the city of Evanston, IL, Demond Mills received Jesus Christ as his Lord and Savior in his youth and answered the call of God to become a minister of the Gospel Jesus Christ in 1997.

Being in ministry for over sixteen years, Demond began serving in prison ministry and later Founded Fresh Start Ministries. Shortly thereafter, he took the gospel to the streets with the mission of winning souls for Jesus Christ. During this time Demond evangelized and prayed for others throughout the local community, which in turn lead to various speaking engagements.

In 2012, Demond and his wife Debra were ordained to the pastorate and led to establish Green Beret Church International in Skokie, IL.

The Lord has put a passion and burden in

Pastor Demond's heart to see people restored, living an abundant life and walking in victory. His mandate is to rebuild the region through prayer, pull down territorial strongholds and take the gospel to the nation. He is a passionate kingdom leader and a great man of warfare, operating in the "Green Beret anointing". Being "a sniper in the spirit," he's not afraid to challenge the kingdom of darkness. Pastor Demond has an apostolic and prophetic call on his life. He moves prophetically as a modern day seer, operating in dreams, visions, interpretations and wisdom.

Apostle Demond is a resident of Skokie, IL with his wife Pastor Debra and their two children Odyssey and Genesis.

He is a licensed and ordained minister under the Apostolic Network of Abiding Presence International Alliance.

Website: www.greenberetministries.com